Animals in the Wild

Antelop

by Mary Hoffman

Belitha Press Limited, London
in association with Methuen Children's Books

There are about eighty different kinds of antelope. These are baby pronghorns from North America. Pronghorn antelopes are the only ones that grow new horns every year. Pronghorns often have twins.

Most antelopes have one calf at a time,
like this springbok from southern Africa.
For the first few weeks of its life, the calf lies
hidden and its mother comes to feed it.

But the calf soon grows stronger and then it goes everywhere with its mother. These are Defassa waterbuck from Kenya. Like all antelopes, they eat mainly grass.

All grazing animals need to move around. As they finish up all the grass in one place, they have to move on to another. They do this in herds because that is safer than travelling alone.

All the antelopes can run fast over short distances.
They need to, in order to escape from large predators like lions and cheetahs.
These are gemsbok from south west Africa.

Another thing that most antelopes do well is leap! This is a female impala and antelopes like her are the best at long-jump. They can cover up to nine metres in one leap.

Some kinds of antelope don't just eat grass. This greater kudu is eating the flowers of an acacia tree. It will eat all kinds of flowers and fruit – even tree bark. This is called browsing.

And there is one antelope that goes even further! This is the gerenuk, from eastern Africa. It often stands up on its hind legs to reach the top branches of trees and shrubs.

All antelopes like to drink a lot, but some spend most of their time in the water. These are reedbuck in a lake in Kenya.

The lechwe likes to feed in the water, but it never goes in too deep because it might need to get out in a hurry! Other antelopes only come to the water for a drink.

Male antelopes often fight using their horns. These elands are trying to prove which is the stronger one. They rub their horns in mud, then tangle them together and push.

After such a fight, the winner chases the loser away. It is only the males who fight. They do it to defend their territory and to keep other males away from "their" females.

The topi is standing on a termite mound, to keep an eye on his territory. This might be as large as 400 hectares and contain up to twenty females.

Male and female antelopes often look different.
These are nyalas and, as you can see,
the females have no horns. Females are
generally smaller than males and lighter in colour.

This blackbuck lives in India. Like many antelopes, its horns grow in a spiral. The horns of antelopes are permanent – if they break one, they can't grow another to replace it.

This is a scimitar-horned oryx of north Africa. When it stands sideways it sometimes looks as if it has only one horn. Some people think this is where the idea of the unicorn comes from.

Gazelles are small kinds of antelope.
They are slender with long legs and necks.
There are lots of them in Africa and many of them are eaten by the big cats.

Completely different from the elegant gazelle
is the wildebeeste, but it is a kind of antelope.
This is a white-bearded wildebeeste,
which is also called a gnu. It lives in Kenya.

In summer, the grass dries up and the herds of wildebeeste travel west across the Mara river, to find fresh grass. Some very old and very young ones die on the crossing and become food for vultures.

Although they are easily startled, some antelopes can be tamed. This man is feeding a mountain gazelle. Large numbers of antelopes used to be killed by big game hunters but now there are laws to protect them.

Index

blackbuck	18
calves	2-4
Defassa waterbuck	4
eland	14
feeding	4-5, 8-9, 11
fighting	14-15
gazelle	20, 23
gemsbok	6, back cover
gerenuk	9
gnu (see wildebeeste)	
greater kudu	8
horns	2, 14, 17, 18, 19
impala	7, 15
kob	front cover
lechwe	11
nyala	17
pronghorn	title page, 2
reedbuck	10
scimitar-horned oryx	19
springbok	3, 5, 12-13
topi	16
wildebeeste	21-22

Useful words about antelopes

to browse	to eat the leaves of a shrub or a tree
bull	a male antelope
calf	a baby antelope, sometimes called a fawn
cow	a female antelope
to graze	to eat grass
predator	an animal which kills other animals for food
ungulate	a mammal with hooves

Dedicated to Camilla

First published 1987 by Belitha Press Limited, 31 Newington Green, London N16 9PU in association with Methuen Children's Books Ltd, 11 New Fetter Lane, London EC4 4EE

Scientific Adviser: Dr Gwynne Vevers. Picture Researcher: Stella Martin. Design: Ken Hatherley
Acknowledgements are due to the following for the photographs used in this book: Bruce Coleman Ltd pp. 2, 3, 9, 12-13 and front cover; Frank Lane Picture Agency pp. 1, 14 and 23; Survival Anglia Ltd pp. 4, 6, 8, 10, 17 and 22; NHPA pp. 7, 18 and back cover; Oxford Scientific Films Ltd p. 11; Natural Science Photos pp. 15, 19, 20 and 21; Eric Hosking p. 16.

ISBN 0 416 01712 6 Printed in Hong Kong by South China Printing Co.